Vol 4

MAZE

Ages 4-6

FOR KIDS

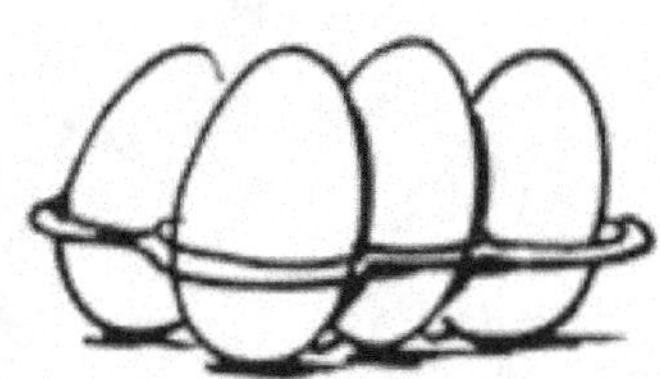

MAZE BOOK

f /MySweetBooks1

t /MySweetBooks1

ig /MySweetBooks1

p /MySweetBooks

Email Us : mysweetbooks1@gmail.com

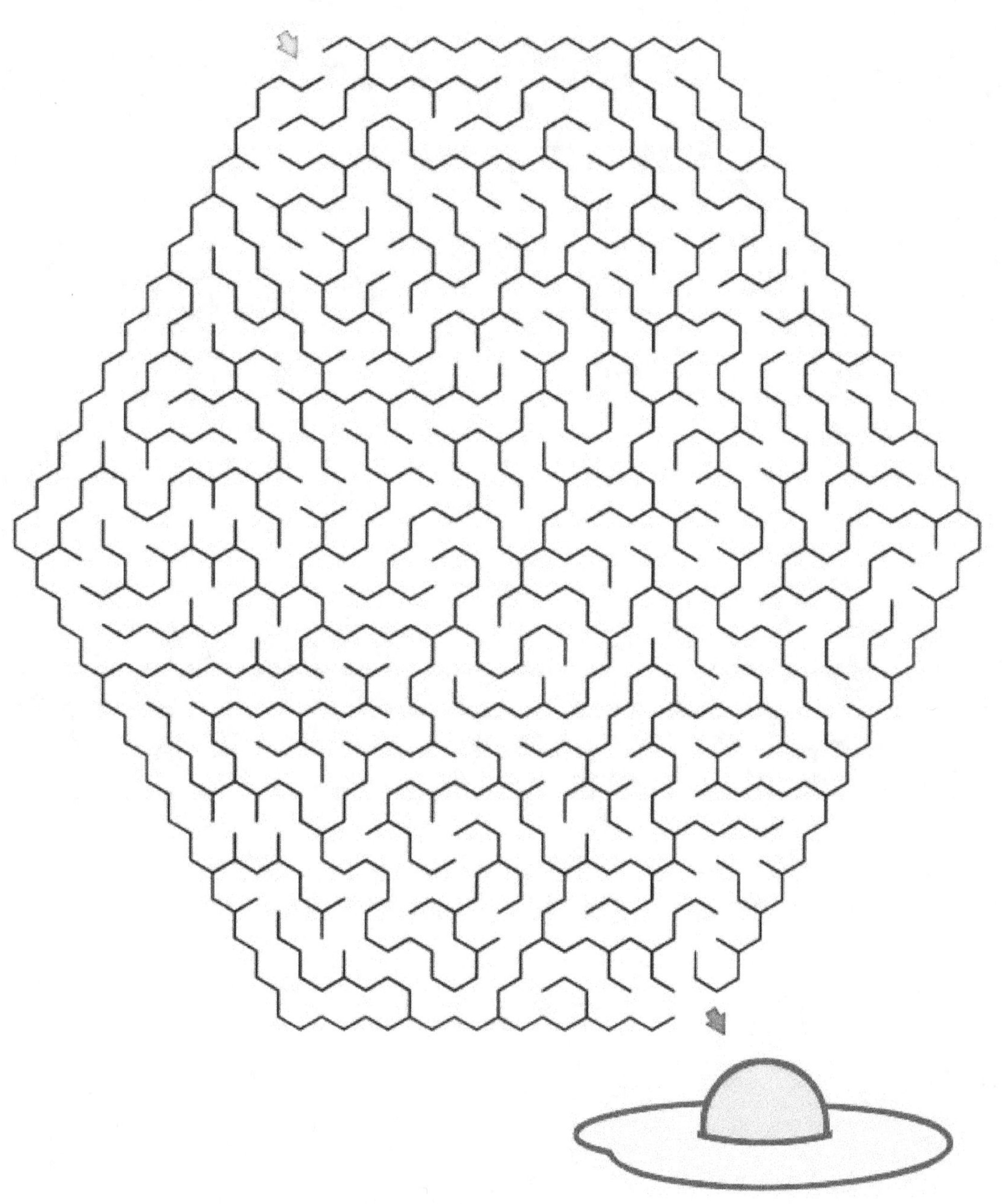

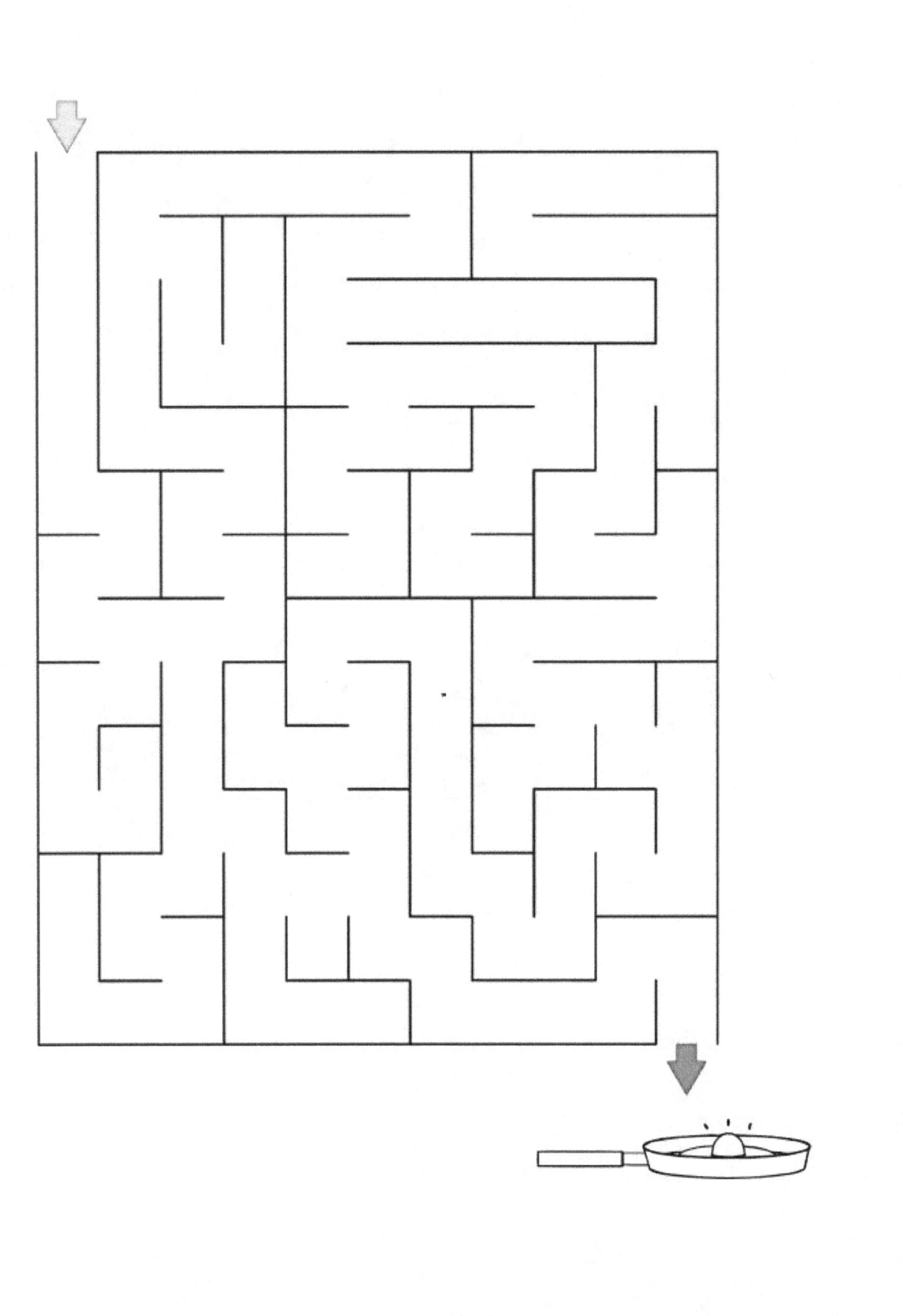

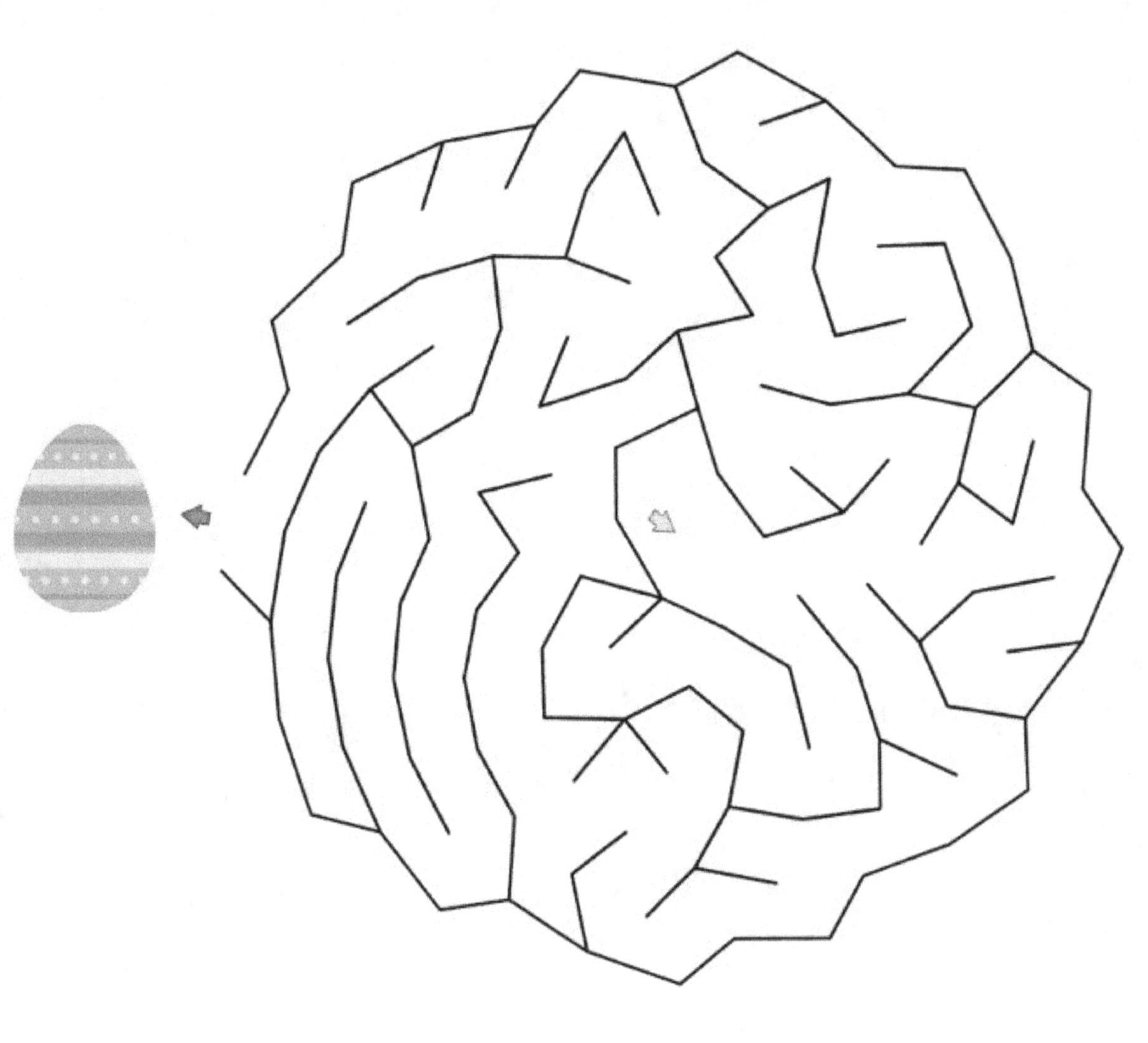

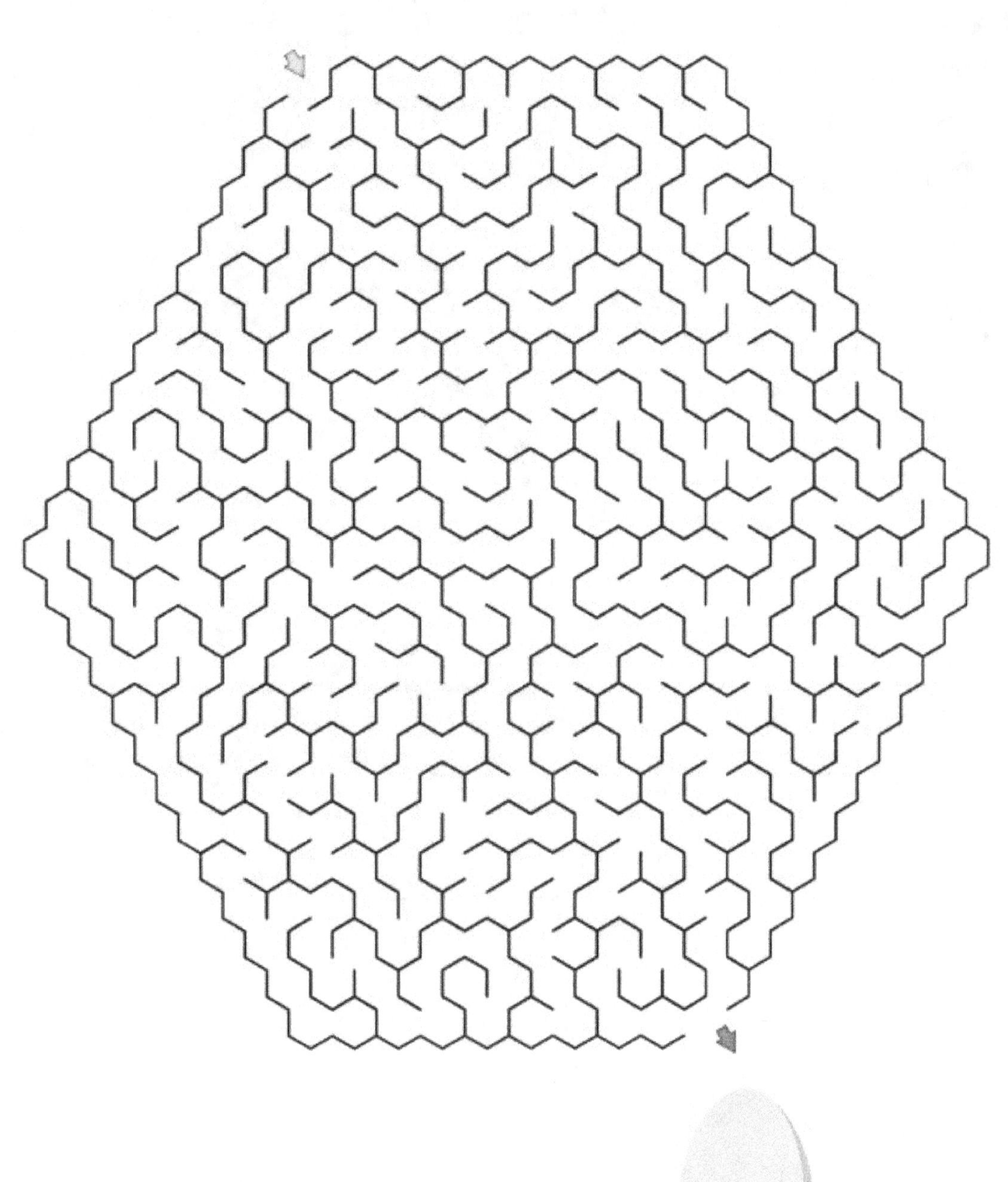

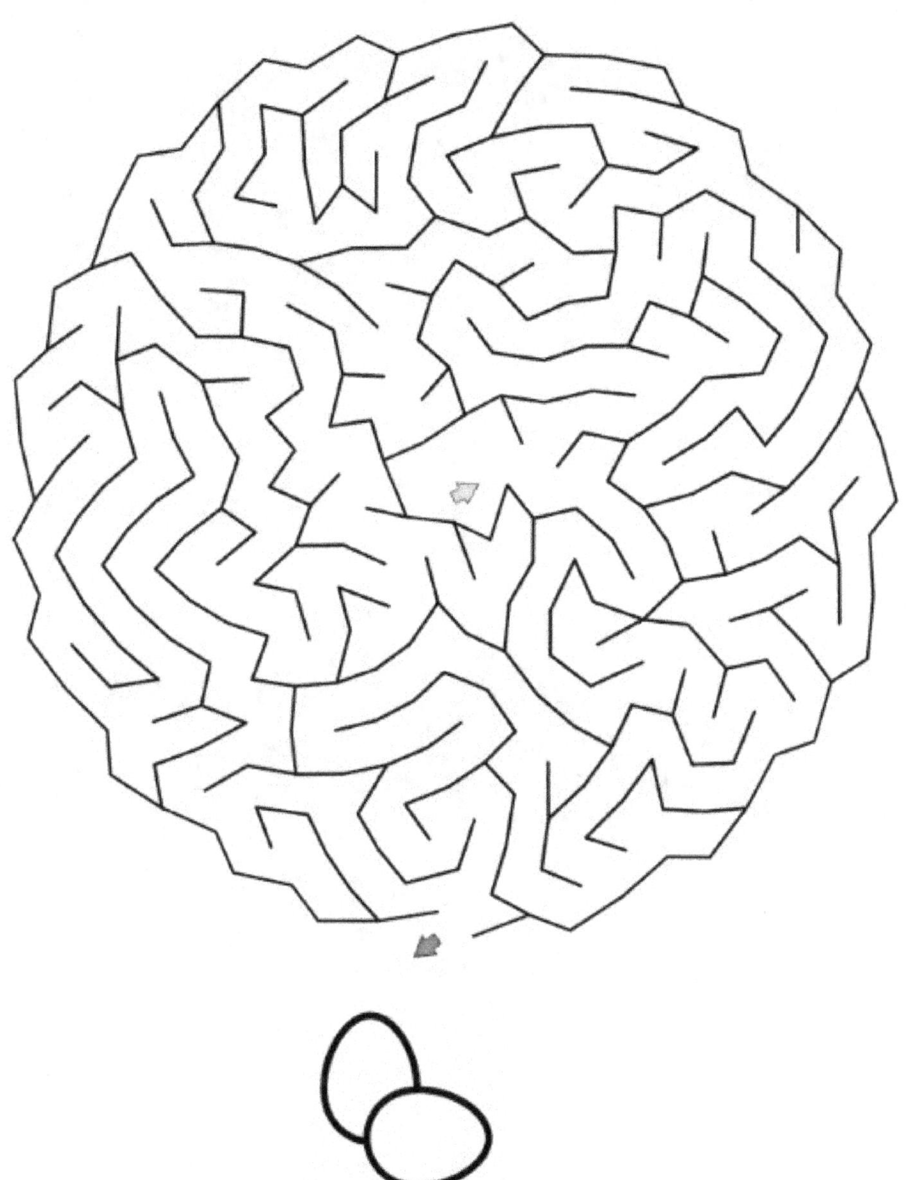

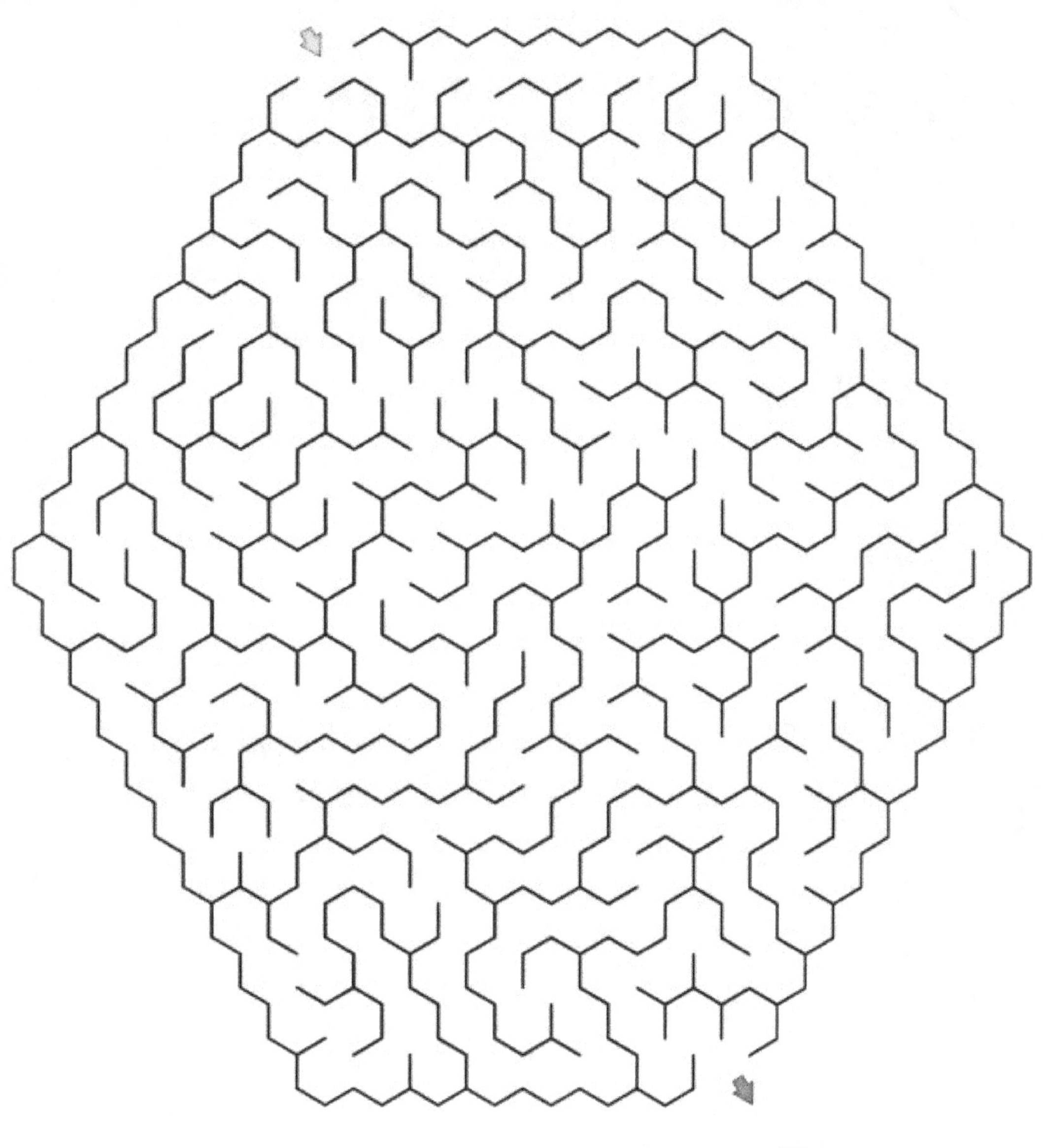

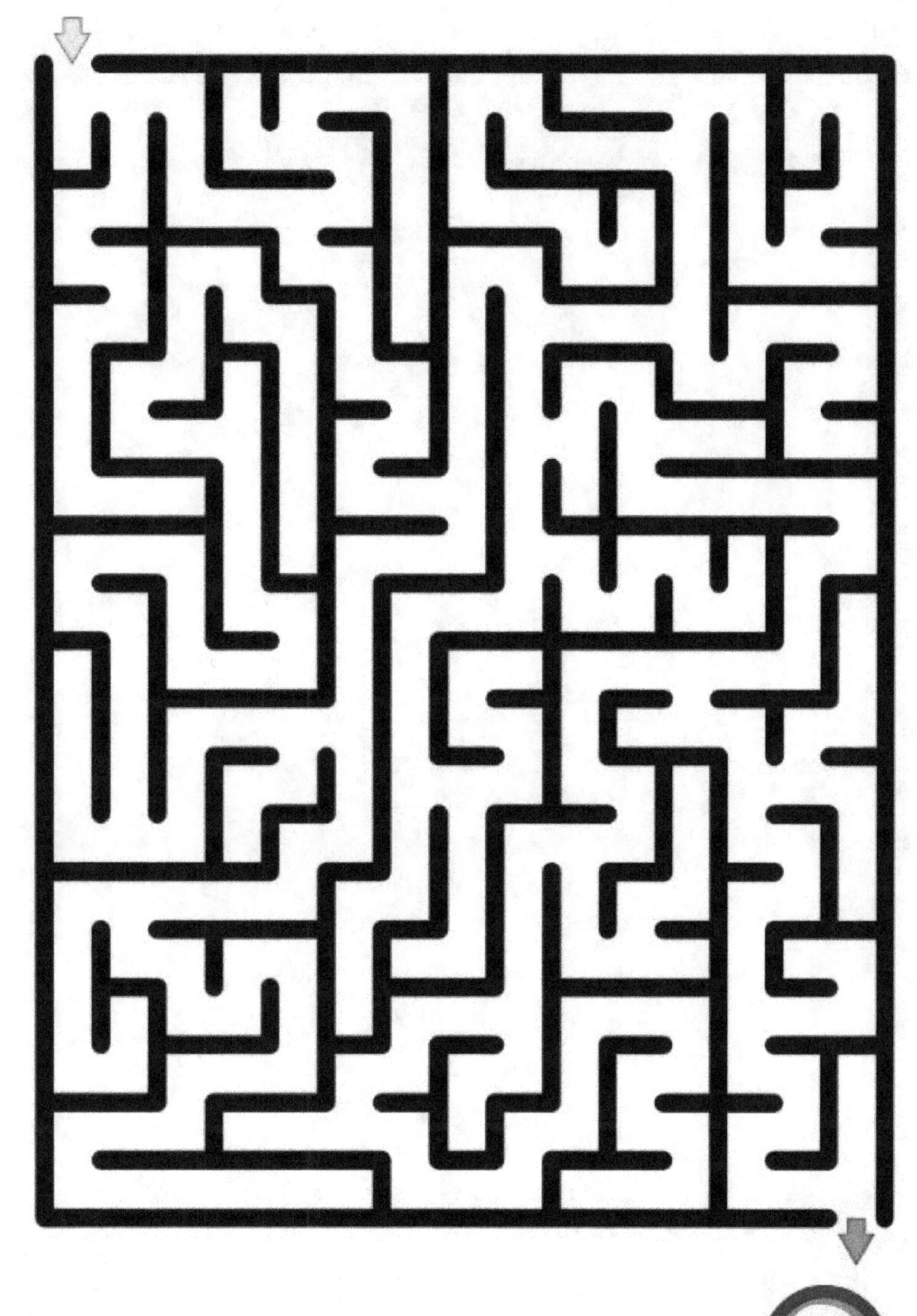

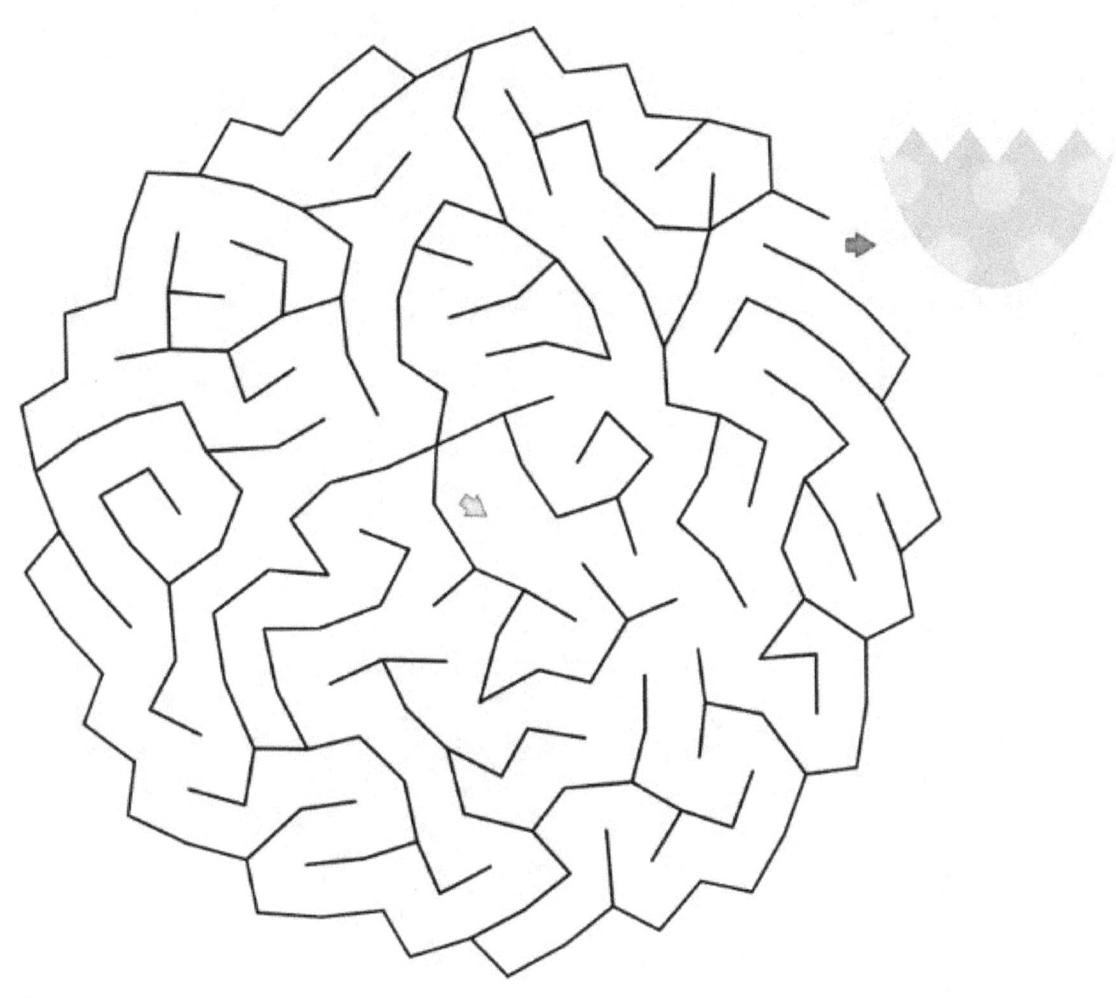

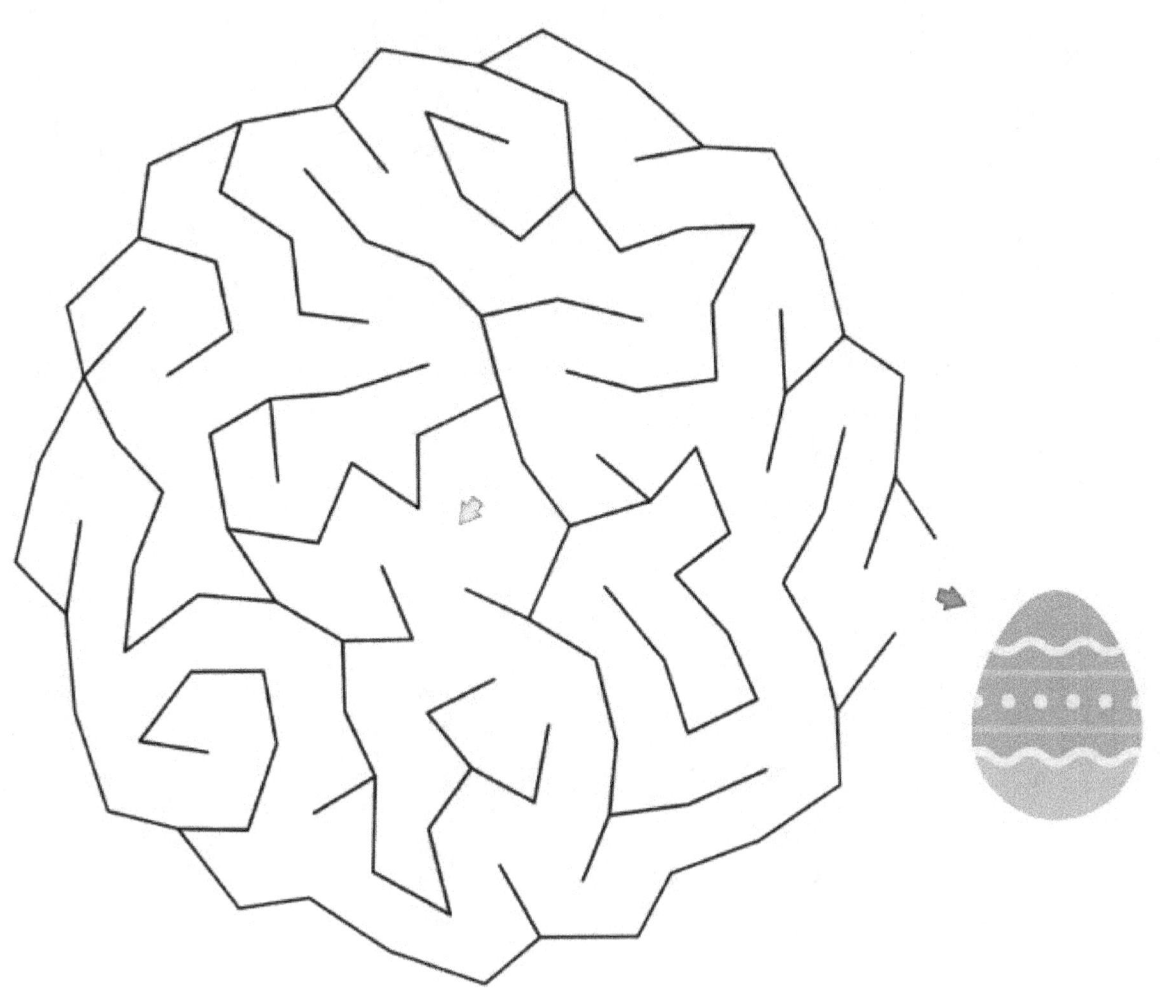

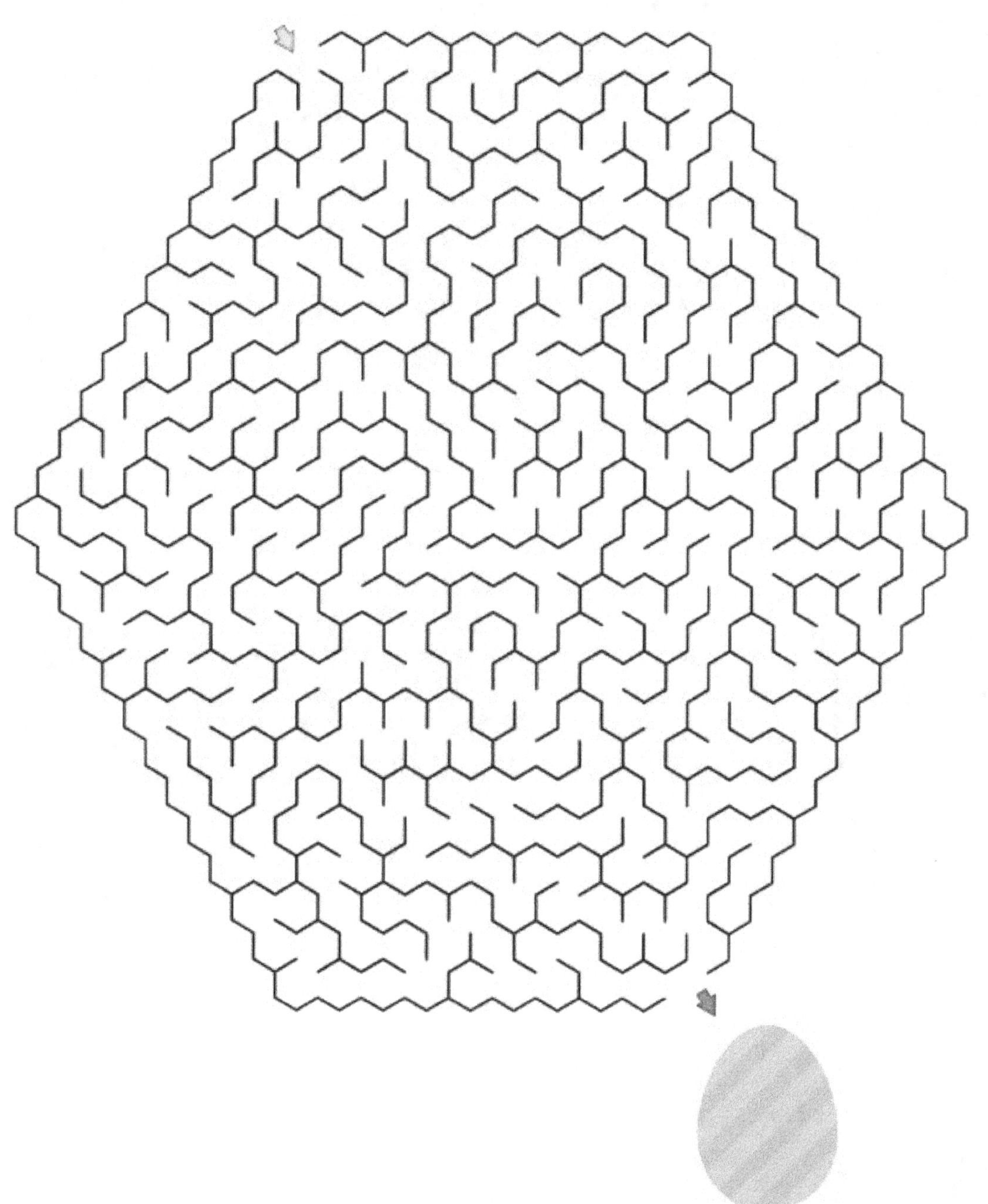

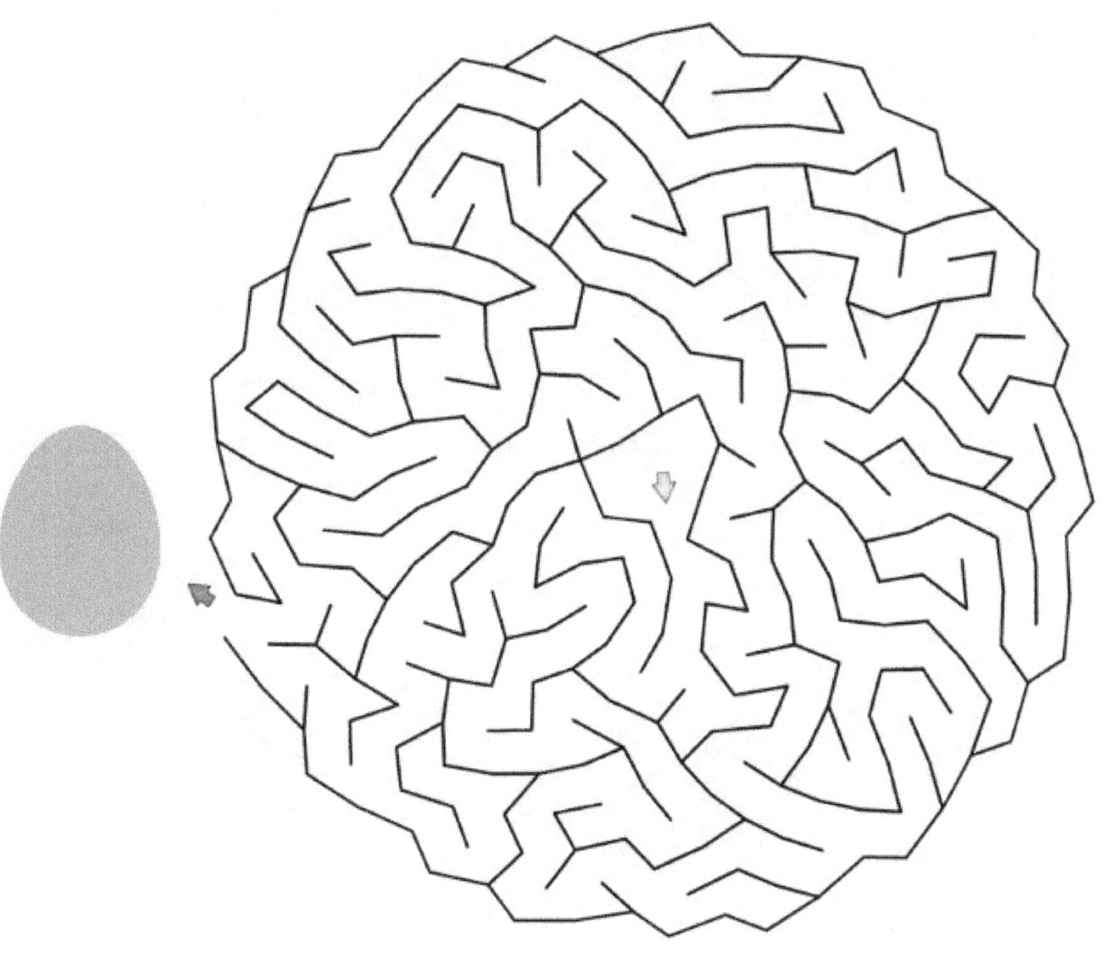